The Break-In

TISH COHEN

The Break-In

Grass Roots Press

First published in 2012 by Grass Roots Press

Grass Roots Press gratefully acknowledges the financial support for its publishing programs provided by the following agencies: the Government of Canada through the Canada Book Fund and the Government of Alberta through the Alberta Foundation for the Arts.

Alberta
Foundation
for the Arts

Grass Roots Press would also like to thank ABC Life Literacy Canada for their support. Good Reads® is used under licence from ABC Life Literacy Canada.

Library and Archives Canada Cataloguing in Publication

Cohen, Tish, 1963–
     The break-in / Tish Cohen.

(Good reads series)
ISBN 978–1–926583–82–2

     1. Readers for new literates. I. Title.
II. Series: Good reads series (Edmonton, Alta.)

PS8605.O3787B74 2012   428.6'2   C2012–902309–4

Printed and bound in Canada.

For Max and Lucas

Chapter One

Alex watched a cricket creep along the baseboard and disappear. He didn't feel strong enough to go after it. Not today. Besides, why try? Seven more crickets were on the loose, and he'd lost the plastic lunch bag they came in.

He sat with his elbows on his knees. His suit jacket didn't fit anymore. It bunched up and hurt him under his arms. All around him, grown-ups sipped tea and ate tiny sandwiches and cookies. As if he couldn't hear them, they whispered about the tragedy. Of course it was a tragedy. Alex's dad was the best police constable on the force, everyone said so. Two days ago, he had stopped a guy for speeding. While he was writing the ticket, another driver hit and killed him. Who could imagine anything worse? Not his son, that's for sure.

"Poor fellow was too young to die," a woman said. Alex knew her; she worked at the main desk of the police station. "Barely fifty. Makes no sense."

The constable beside her nodded. "That's the thing about life. Does its best to mess us up."

Alex hated this little house on Poplar Avenue. Everything about it was bad. His dad had wanted to live closer to work. That's why the family had moved here from the other side of town a month ago. Four crappy weeks. In that time, Alex had had two teeth filled and his mother had had the stomach flu. Now his dad was dead. Loose crickets didn't matter compared to that.

His mother looked sadder and taller than ever in her borrowed funeral dress. "Honey," she said, "you need to eat." She held out a plate of salad.

Alex stared at the lettuce, making a face.

"You need to keep your strength up."

Using the smallest amount of air he could, Alex said, "L-l-lettuce is for c-c … crickets."

His mother's hand went to her throat and started to play with her pearl necklace. His stutter was getting to her. She couldn't handle that it had come back after three years. Alex felt guilty as hell. His mother didn't need to worry about her son not being able to speak, on top of everything else.

Alex flipped a piece of lettuce behind the sofa. "B-b-b-b … b-bait."

"Did the whole bag of crickets escape? Or just a few?"

He didn't answer.

"Alex, how many crickets escaped?"

He just shook his head. Knowing that eight crickets were loose in her house wasn't going to make her feel better.

"I still don't understand why I had to buy you a pet spider right now," Alex's mother said. "You can't even hug it and get any sort of comfort."

Alex stared at the ceiling. How many times did he have to tell her? The Mexican palomino spider was *not* poisonous. Well, not very poisonous. Boris the spider's bite was something like a bee sting. He was extremely gentle and easy to handle. And— bonus!—his hair didn't give humans a rash, like the hair of some spiders did. No itching. No killer biting.

"He's not p-p-p …" Alex tried to let the word escape. "Not p … p …"

His mom's sadness made her face droop. "It's the stress of what happened. Losing Dad. You'll feel better once you get back to your old routine. That's what you need."

That wasn't what he needed. What he needed was to get back at the guy who killed his father.

Sergeant Hines walked across the room with a black box in his hand. He sat in the chair next to Alex while Alex's mother watched, wiping her nose with a tissue. At the funeral, Alex's dad's police hat had been placed on the coffin. Then, at the end of the funeral, the sergeant gave the hat to Alex's mom, the widow. She'd cried. Man, had she cried.

"A few things from your dad's desk," Sergeant Hines said to Alex as he opened the box. The World's Best Dad mug Alex had given his dad for Father's Day. A framed picture of Alex with his parents in front of the fireplace in their old home. An award for bravery.

Alex said, "W-w-w-what d-d-d …?"

The sergeant leaned closer. "What's that?"

Alex's mom answered for him. "He wants to know what his dad did. For the award."

"Took on an armed suspect all by himself during a home invasion. Saved a young mother and her three little ones. Your dad was quite the cop, Alex. He will be sadly missed."

The sergeant meant to make him feel better, but Alex only felt worse.

His mom took the box and held it to her chest. Alex could see she was blinking back tears. "Thank you, Sergeant."

"I know who d-d-did i-i-i … who d-did it."

Sergeant Hines smiled sadly. "Who would that be, son?"

A good cop looks at the clues. The hit-and-run driver who killed Alex's dad left almost none. Only chips of dark red paint on the door of the car Alex's dad had pulled over. The guy getting the ticket couldn't describe the other driver's car. All he knew was that it was an old red clunker.

Old Man Morrison, Alex's one and only suspect, lived across the street. He and Alex were enemies. As the new boy at school, Alex got picked on, of course. Two weeks ago, bullies had stolen his backpack. Alex couldn't care less about his school books, but in his backpack he'd had a bendable pen from Disneyland. Now he'd never get it back. The day after the bullies took his backpack, Alex saw them again. To get away, he cut through Old Man Morrison's yard.

Morrison had trimmed his shrubs into crazy shapes: a swan, a giraffe, a rocket ship. He was nuts about those bushes. He threw a fit when Alex cut through his yard. Alex, he said, had broken some of the lower branches. He demanded that Alex fix them. Which was impossible. How do you put a broken branch back together?

Alex's dad went to calm the guy down, even offered to pay him, but Morrison wouldn't listen. He said he'd get even. That alone didn't make the old man a suspect. But this did: Morrison drove a very old, very red clunker.

Alex decided to tell Sergeant Hines the name of his suspect. "M-M-Morr ..."

"Excuse me?"

"He thinks Mr. Morrison, across the street, did it," said Alex's mom. "He drives a red car."

"*O-o-old* red car."

The sergeant, like about ten other people that day, tapped Alex under his chin. "Every dark red car is being looked at. If the paint matches, we'll be talking to Mr. Morrison in the next few days. Don't you worry."

But Morrison could leave town. Every good cop knows the bad guy will try to run. "In the next few days" wasn't soon enough. Alex shook his head angrily.

The sergeant leaned close and smiled. "You just leave the policing to the police. You're the man of the house now, son. It's up to you to take care of things around here." He stood up to leave, and a puzzled look crossed his face. "Do I hear a cricket?"

Chapter Two

The next morning, Marcus sat across from his doctor and rubbed at his new beard. Strange that it took him until age twenty-seven to finally grow a bit of hair on his face. He wondered if stress could do that. Make a person hairier.

Dr. Ling yawned into her hand. "Excuse me," she said as she opened his file.

He leaned back into his chair and tried not to yawn back. He'd had a bad night. Didn't fall asleep until three or four o'clock. Then he slept through his alarm and raced out the door without even showering. He didn't want to be late for therapy. It was all that was keeping him sane since Lisa walked out.

The doctor looked up. "You were starting to tell me about your sadness. How you're coping with it."

Marcus looked down at the photo in his hand. It was taken three years ago, back when he and Lisa were in their last year of art college. God, she was beautiful. Her freckles, her wavy brown hair. It blew across her face and got in her mouth. That drove her nuts. She was so pretty it wasn't fair. No one could hold on to such a woman. And no one could get over her once she was gone.

They'd been living together. Planning to get married. To move down to Australia, where he could surf and she could paint sunrises. They would take a few years off from career-type goals. Work in a beach bar, mixing fancy drinks. Find themselves. That was the plan. It wasn't a plan their parents loved, but that didn't matter. All that mattered was each other.

Everything changed a couple of months back. Marcus had still been working at the liquor store. One day, he came home to find Lisa's things gone from their tiny house on Poplar Avenue. Not just her clothes and makeup, either. She had really cleaned the place out. She took the sticky, half-empty shampoo bottles from the back of the bathroom cupboard. She even took the hair dryer. That dryer could kill a person. You had to unplug it when you left the room because it sparked even when it was off.

What could he do? He sobbed into his pillow for a day, or ten. Then he realized he couldn't possibly afford to rent the house all by himself. So he, too, moved out. Moved in with his mother, back into the bedroom he slept in when he was a child. Where he could sob into the pillow of his childhood for another day, or ten.

Finally, his mother suggested that he go for therapy.

"Marcus?" said Dr. Ling. "Can you tell me about your sadness—how it feels?"

"It's kind of stupid."

"Nothing is stupid in this office. I promise."

"I feel like I'm not even here. Ever since Lisa left, I feel like I'm on the outside of life. Like I'm watching from the corner, you know?" Dr. Ling shifted in her chair. "This sadness is so bad I can no longer work. I don't sleep."

Dr. Ling nodded.

"Sometimes it feels, well, it feels almost like …
you're going to think this is weird," Marcus said.

"I won't think anything you say is weird,
Marcus. I promise."

Marcus felt his cheeks heat up. "Okay. This
sadness, it's almost as if the stinging lives in my
skin. When I think of her, my entire body feels as
if it's covered in paper cuts. I would do anything to
stop the pain. I have to get her back."

"I thought we agreed the other day that Lisa
isn't good for you," said Dr. Ling.

Marcus hadn't agreed to anything the other
day. His skin had just hurt too much for him to set
the doctor straight. "That's not true," he said now.
A garbage truck outside made a whining sound.
Trash cans smashed together like thunder. The
noise made Marcus feel brave. "I'd take Lisa back
in a second. Any man would. She's perfect."

Dr. Ling checked her watch. "I'm afraid our
time is up for today." She stood up. "Some things
we can't change, Marcus. You'll learn as you get
older that life is going to happen, whether we like it
or not. Sometimes we get scratched up, sometimes
we don't. The best we can do is learn how to cope
and soldier through."

Chapter Three

Like Marcus, Alex had a hard time getting up that morning. He lay in bed and pretended not to feel his mother shaking his shoulder.

"Alex, wake up," he heard.

He opened his eyes and stared at Boris's tank. The spider was pawing at the glass almost as if he were waving hello. Even with the silky blond hair, Boris was terrifying. Of course, terrifying was the point.

"You don't want to be late for school."

What was Alex supposed to do? Get up, pull on his jeans and sweatshirt, and get on the bus, as if everything was fine? Nothing was fine. Nothing would be fine ever again. His dad was dead, his dad's killer was free, and Alex was in charge of the family.

"I'm s-s-s …" He stopped, shook his head, frustrated. "I'm s … s …"

"It's okay, honey. It's been a tough few days."

He rolled his eyes back and stuck his tongue out one side of his mouth.

"You're sick?" His mother put a hand on his forehead. "You don't have a fever. You seem to be fine."

Not on the inside, he didn't say.

She stood up. "Okay. But I have to go to work. You'll have to fend for yourself. Know what that means?"

Cereal for every meal. He nodded.

"And maybe you'll try to gather up some of those bugs before they get into the walls. Those beetles chirped all night long."

Crickets, he didn't say.

"Otherwise we'll have to call in a pest control guy. Remember Grandpa's snails?"

Alex's dad had told him a story about his grandfather. Back in the 1950s, Grandpa and his three brothers ran a fruit and vegetable store. One day, Grandpa had a great idea. The store already sold unusual foods, like avocados and purple potatoes. "Classy restaurants serve snails now,"

Grandpa said to his brothers. "Escargots, they call them. We should get some snails to sell."

"Snails?" his brothers said in horror. "We're not investing a single dollar in snails."

But Grandpa was certain he was onto something big. He ordered the snails anyway from a snail farmer in northern Africa. A few weeks later, on a hot day, three long, narrow containers arrived at his house. They looked like giant baskets with lids, and each weighed about as much as a ten-year-old child.

But Grandpa had a problem. The snails had to be kept in a cool place, like the cellar. But there was no way he could get the containers down the stairs. So he had a bright idea. He put the snails in paper grocery bags and taped the tops shut. Then he set bag after bag on the cellar floor. In the morning, he would drive them to restaurants and sell them. He figured he'd make about $2,000. If his brothers didn't want to share in it, that was their loss.

The next day, Grandpa dressed in his best suit. Then he went down to the cellar to collect his little money-makers. When he turned on the light, the bags were gone. He looked around and saw snails everywhere—on the dirt floor, up the shelves, on the ceiling. The entire cellar was wiggling with snails.

Turned out, snails ate paper.

Yesterday, Alex had made Grandpa's mistake. He thought that an air-filled plastic bag was a safe home for his crickets.

Turned out, crickets ate through plastic.

"I'll f-f-f …"

"I know, sweetie. You'll find them." She stood up and playfully shook a finger at him. "You behave, hear me?"

He cupped a hand to his ear as if he didn't hear her.

"Very funny. See you at five-thirty." She pulled on her jacket and headed for the door. "School tomorrow, for sure."

He didn't look up.

"Alex?"

He rolled over and faced the wall.

Her voice was soft now. "Staying home won't bring your father back, sweetheart."

So far, the morning had been pretty decent, Alex decided. He'd put his baseball cards in order. He'd watched cartoons. He'd even filled Boris's drinking sponge with water. Now it was after eleven o'clock, and he hadn't even had breakfast. With his stomach growling, he grabbed a carton of milk and the Life cereal. Then he reached into the cupboard and took out two bowls.

He stopped. Stared at the bowls.

It had been their routine. Every morning, while his dad was shaving, Alex poured the cereal and set it on the table. His dad would finally arrive in the kitchen, still buttoning his police shirt or smoothing wet hair. Only then did Alex pour the milk. With cereal, you couldn't pour the milk too early. The cereal had to be soft, but not too soft.

Alex put the bowls away. Cereal at lunch time was a lousy idea anyway.

What he really needed to do was find at least one of the escaped crickets for Boris's next meal. Not that the spider would be hungry just yet. He'd had a cricket yesterday, before the great cricket escape. He didn't really need to eat for another week, but Alex wanted him to keep his strength up.

Standing in the hallway, Alex tried to imagine where he'd go if he were a cricket. He glanced at the open window in the living room. Outside, that's where he'd go. Especially if he knew he was meant to be food for a big, hairy spider.

He looked closely at the window for signs of a cricket break-out. But nothing had chewed through the screen. There wasn't a crack wide enough for a cricket to wiggle through, either. Which was a good sign. It meant the crickets might be in the house still.

The room smelled of fresh paint, even now.

The day before they'd moved in, his father had woken him when it was still dark. "Do you want to have a great experience?" he had asked.

Alex had pulled on his jeans and jumped in the car. His dad explained their plan as they drove. "We're going to surprise Mom. You know how she loves the ocean? We're going to paint the front rooms in the new house a nice pale blue."

"Painting," Alex had said. "Is that the 'great experience'?"

"No," his dad replied.

Just as the sky started to brighten with morning sun, they pulled into a Tim Hortons drive-through. Alex asked for hot chocolate, but his dad shook his head. He bought them each a coffee and a muffin. They could eat the muffin, his dad said. But they couldn't touch the coffee. Was this the "great experience"? Again, his dad said no.

The car came to a stop in the parking lot of the big hardware store. Coffee in hand, they walked inside, Alex watching for signs of a great experience.

Finally, they stood facing aisle 6B. It was lined to the ceiling with cans of latex and oil paint. Professional painters in beat-up, paint-splattered white overalls studied the selection. Alex's dad looked at him and nodded. Coffee time. Alex sipped and made a face—the coffee was screaming hot and tasted bitter and burnt. Anyway, he followed his dad down the paint aisle. They walked past the guy with big muscles and a gold hoop earring. Past the two skinny ones, old enough to be grandfathers, arguing about which beige their customer wanted. And past the young woman taking photos of paint samples with her cell phone.

At the end of the aisle, Alex's dad stopped. Waved back toward all of the painters. They all had coffee.

Finally, Alex understood. Up early, coffee in hand, at the hardware store getting ready for an honest day's work. He and his dad had been part of something that morning.

Anyway. Today the paint smell made his stomach hurt. There was too much of his father in this house.

He tried to pull the couch away from the wall so he could check on yesterday's lettuce. See if any crickets had taken the bait. The sofa was heavier than he expected; he couldn't move it very far. He squeezed down behind it, feeling around in the dark for the lettuce. Or, even better, but far less likely, an actual cricket. But the lettuce was gone. Which was a good sign. It meant the crickets were alive and well.

As he backed himself out from behind the sofa, his hand fell on something small and hard. He closed his fist around it.

It was a brass bullet. From his dad's old .32 calibre Smith & Wesson, the one he used for target practice on days off. A revolver, with a bullet chamber that turned every time the gun was fired. His dad often unloaded the revolver on the living room table. He was always careful, but this bullet clearly escaped.

Alex slid it into his pocket.

Chapter Four

When Marcus got home from Dr. Ling's office, he crawled back into bed. What else did he have to do? At least when he was asleep he didn't have to think about Lisa.

He was up again, just stepping out of the shower, when the doorbell rang. Figured. The one time he didn't bring his clothes into the bathroom.

The bell rang again. Marcus dried off a bit and rushed to the door, wrapping the towel around his waist.

The last person he expected to see was Lisa. But there she stood on the porch, sunlight creating a halo behind her head. The way she was dressed told Marcus that she was on her way either to or from the gym. To, Marcus decided. Her fluffy hair showed that she hadn't worked out yet. This was a girl who put her heart into everything. When she was done at the gym, she looked like she'd just dragged herself out of a puddle. Dripping wet and worn out. But still beautiful.

"Wow." He tried not to grin. "This is a surprise."

"How's it going?"

"Good." He pulled the towel tighter around his waist and waved her into the house. "Come, sit. I'll just get dressed."

"Is your mother home?"

"No, she's at work. We're all alone."

"Good." Lisa walked into the living room as proudly as Queen Elizabeth herself. "I don't have long."

Marcus excused himself and dug through his dresser for a T-shirt. When he'd moved home, he hadn't taken much care with unpacking. He had wadded up most of his clothes and stuffed them into drawers made for children's clothes. He pulled on the least wrinkled shirt he could find and a pair of jeans. Lisa loved him in jeans.

Hair still dripping, he sank into the chair across from her. He smiled, frozen by the pressure of the moment. He needed to say something clever, something to impress her. Something to make her desperate to have him back in her life. But all he came up with was, "Wow. You look great."

"Thanks."

"How've you been?"

She tucked her hair behind her ears and glanced around the room. "Did you see my good ring in your boxes after you moved out of the Poplar Avenue house? I can't find it."

"*Going Home* is playing at the Empire Theatre. Have you heard of it? Getting great reviews."

"I really need the ring back, Marcus. Have you unpacked everything?"

"What? Yes. Which ring—your grandma's emerald?"

"Yeah. I'm thinking it might be above the medicine cabinet in the bathroom," Lisa said. "Remember? I hid it there so no robber could find it."

"Why don't you knock on the door and ask the new people to look?"

"I already went. This lady answered and she had all these rings—one on every finger. You know what that means."

"No," Marcus admitted.

Lisa sighed. "It means she's a ring person. So I know exactly what would happen. She'd go look, find it, stick it in her pocket. She'd come back to the door all, 'Sorry, I couldn't find any ring.'"

"I don't know about that …"

Lisa shifted forward on the sofa cushion and peered toward the kitchen. "You're sure your mom is at work?"

"Yes."

"Okay. I have an idea. It involves you."

Here was Lisa, asking him for help. It was like a dream.

"I still have my key," she said. "I'll give it to you. Then you drive back to the house and get the ring while they're all at work."

He squinted at her. "Wait—you want me to break in?"

"Not break in. Just go get my ring. There's no law against going and getting something you forgot."

"There is when it's inside a house you don't live in anymore."

She tugged her hair out of her ponytail and messed up the front so it fell in front of her cheekbones. Then she looked up at him with those crazy greyish-purple eyes. "Please?"

"Lisa. Let's be real. We could speak to the landlord, and he'll—"

"If we do that, *he'll* pocket the ring. Don't you see how easy this will be? You open the door. You walk into the bathroom. You get me my ring, and then …" Lisa paused to smile at him the way he adored, with her lower teeth showing. She shrugged with one shoulder. "And then, who knows?"

He thought about this for a moment. What did she mean, "who knows"? That they'd get back together?

"I'd really, really appreciate it."

"It's just that it's illegal. Break and enter."

She set the key on the table and pushed it toward him. "You'd be in and out in less than a minute."

"It takes me longer than that to untie my shoes."

"You're not taking your shoes off, for god's sakes!"

"What if I get caught?" Marcus said. "I could go to jail."

"How are you going to get caught? You're walking in with a key. And the neighbours are used to seeing you."

"Yeah, they'll wonder why I'm walking into the new people's place!"

"No one notices their neighbours. Everyone's too busy with their own crap. Come on, Marcus. Life is messy. You have to deal."

Life is messy. Just like Dr. Ling said. Marcus reached for the key and stood up. "All right. I'll go get your ring back." He closed his eyes as she kissed his cheek.

Maybe, just maybe, he'd get his life back, too.

An hour later, Marcus brought his rusted black Civic to a stop on Poplar Avenue. He'd been calm the whole way over. His mother had left him a grocery list, and he'd been clear-headed enough to stop at the store. But now, with the front door of the house so close, panic rose up his throat.

What if someone saw him? What if Mr. Morrison, across the street, was looking out his window right now? What if he called the police? The guy was crazy. Let the air out of all four of Lisa's tires one morning because she'd parked too close to his driveway. And when Marcus had called him on it, the old guy had laughed. "When you're at work," he said, "your girlfriend entertains other fellas. All of 'em better looking than you." Lisa denied this, of course. Marcus had wished Morrison dead ever since.

A school bus full of children crept past. All the kids had their faces pressed against the window. Staring at him. Probably memorizing the colour of his hair, the space between his eyes, the make of his car. All so they could describe everything to the police, the newspapers. The judge.

Marcus's heart hammered. Then it seemed to skip a beat—held still for a moment, then beat twice. Could a twenty-seven-year-old have a heart attack? He climbed out of the car and leaned against the door. Bent over to slow his breathing. Calm the hell down.

Lisa and Dr. Ling were right. Life was itchy and scratchy. And you didn't get anywhere by hiding from it.

Marcus stood up straight. That was that. He'd forget about neighbours and heart attacks and jail time, and get on with living. He started up the driveway to get the ring.

He'd win his girlfriend back if it killed him.

Chapter Five

———

Standing in front of his parents' closet, Alex pulled on his dad's police shirt. Way too big, but who cared? As he buttoned it, he found himself staring at the big, silver safe on the closet floor. He wasn't allowed to touch it. When there was a gun in the house, there were extra rules. But those rules didn't apply today. His dad was dead and his mom wasn't home.

No one was around to stop him.

The numbers went 71-11-26. His mother's birthday and the combination of the safe. He wasn't supposed to know it, but he did. He'd been reading in his own room, next to theirs, when they brought the safe home from Staples. They hadn't exactly whispered it.

With a few turns of the dial, the safe door swung open. There, under the box of his father's work things that the sergeant had given to Alex, was the gun. And holster.

Never before had he touched them.

He buckled the holster around his waist. Slipped the gun into it. His dad's pilot-style sunglasses winked at him from the dresser. He slid them into his shirt pocket and looked in the mirror. Even with the holster belting it tight, the shirt came almost to his knees. But still. He raised the gun to chest height, pointed it to the ceiling. He squinted as if staring down a bad guy.

He looked awesome. The way he would when he himself was a cop one day.

The ringing phone startled him. With the gun tucked under his arm, he answered without saying hello.

"Alex? How are you doing?" It was his mother.

"F-f-f ..." The gun started to slip and he squeezed his arm tighter to his body. "F-f-f ..."

"You doing okay, little man?"

He nodded.

"I can't hear you. Tap the phone once if you're okay. Twice if you're not."

Tap. The revolver slipped further down his ribs. The gun now pointed at his face. Looking into the barrel was like staring down the black hole of death. He shifted it to point it toward the wall.

"Okay. I was thinking of bringing home hamburgers for dinner."

Silence.

"Once if you're fine with burgers."

Tap.

"And, honey, I really want you to go to school tomorrow."

Silence.

"Honey?"

Silence.

Alex's mother sighed. "Okay. We'll talk about it later. I'll get you onion rings."

Silence.

"Alex, are you still there?"

As Alex tapped, the gun dropped to the floor with a heavy thunk.

"What was that noise?" she said.

Lucky the gun wasn't loaded.

"Alex, are you all right?"

Tap.

"I'll see you tonight, little man."

He tossed the phone onto the bed and pulled the bullet out of his pocket. It slid into the revolver with a satisfying click.

Chapter Six

Marcus pulled the key out of his pocket and prayed it would work. The little house on Poplar Avenue had always had a sticky lock. Lisa used to nag Marcus to spray the keyhole with some sort of oil. Because one time, on a really snowy winter day, she couldn't get in. She and her groceries had to wait on the steps for a half-hour in the howling wind. By the time Marcus got home to jiggle the key the right way, Lisa couldn't feel her toes.

Now Marcus turned the key and bumped the door with his shoulder. The door opened with ease. Hardly daring to breathe, he waited, listened. There were no cars in the driveway, but still. Maybe they didn't have cars, these people. When he was sure nobody was home, he stepped inside. Slipped off his running shoes and set them neatly on the mat. He wasted valuable seconds staring at the new wall colour. A fresh, pale blue. In fact, the whole place looked different. It had something of a home-like feel now. When he and Lisa lived here, the rooms looked less comfortable. Not like a place you stay at for very long. More like a place you stop at on your way to someplace else.

Enough with the daydreams. It was time to act.

As Marcus tiptoed along the hall toward the bathroom, Alex was busy at the back of the house. He dropped the spider back in his tank after trying to give him some exercise. The workout on the foot of his bed had been kind of a bust. Picking up Boris was more horrible than Alex had imagined. All those legs moving at once. Those prickly hairs. The possibility of getting bitten—even by the non-poisonous Boris. As gently as he could, Alex had tossed the spider onto the blanket. Then he spent the next half-hour trying to think how to put Boris back without actually touching him.

In the end, he counted to three, bit down on his tongue to distract himself, and did it. But one thing was certain. He never wanted to touch Boris again.

Which wasn't going to help his plan.

Alex looked out the window at the backyard. A good cop always considers the facts.

Fact one. His dad had been standing at the side of the road.

Fact two. A speeding car had hit both Alex's dad and the door of the silver car he'd pulled over.

Fact three. The hit-and-run car had left dark red paint on the silver car.

Fact four. Dark red was not a popular car colour these days. Why would it be? It looked like dried blood.

Fact five. The accident took place right around the corner. Less than five blocks from home. And right across from home was Mr. Morrison's house. Morrison had an old red Ford Taurus.

Fact six, the most important fact of all. Mr. Morrison wanted revenge.

Alex's dad used to say, you catch the criminals, and they're out on the streets the next week. He'd said it a million times. Even if the police did believe Alex, turning in Morrison wouldn't work, not long term. He had to take care of the guy himself.

He started toward the kitchen for a snack. Before he could work out the details of his plan, he needed to fill his stomach.

Less than halfway down the hall, he heard a noise. A bump. No, not a bump. More of a thud. Or a thunk. Yes, that was it. A thunk. It sounded like it was coming from the bathroom.

He froze. It wasn't even one o'clock. His mother wouldn't leave work until five. Which meant one thing.

Alex was in the middle of a break and enter.

His heart beat so hard he could feel it in his throat. He wanted to run. But to get out, he had to pass the bathroom.

The police sergeant's words echoed in his head. *You're the man of the house now, son. It's up to you to take care of things around here.* Alex knew what that meant. It meant he had to take care of his mother.

His mother—what if she came home early? Walked right into the crime scene? He couldn't lose his only parent.

As quietly as he could, he slipped into the spare bedroom and picked up the phone. Dialled 911. Nothing happened. There was no dial tone, just dead air. Now he remembered. He had just dropped the phone on the bed after his mother called. He hadn't actually hung up.

Which meant he was all alone with the guy who had broken in.

You're the man of the house now ...

What choice did he have? He pulled his dad's revolver out of the holster and crept into the hall. Inching sideways toward the bathroom door.

A clink. The sound of a bottle tipping over. As if someone was putting on makeup or looking for a Band-Aid.

Alex's hands were so sweaty he nearly dropped the gun again. He took a deep breath and lifted one foot to kick open the bathroom door.

Chapter Seven

Marcus stared at the mirror, confused. He'd run his hand across the top of the medicine cabinet. He'd searched inside the medicine cabinet. He'd checked the floor under the medicine cabinet. There was no ring anywhere. It was supposed to be lying on top. That's where Lisa had always kept it.

She wouldn't believe him. She'd think he didn't look in the right place. Or that he knocked the ring into the drain. Maybe down between the wall and the cabinet.

But he'd checked everywhere. The cupboard under the sink, the floor, behind the toilet. The bathroom was tiny. There was nowhere else to search. The ring was gone.

He leaned over the sink to drink from the tap. Just as he stood up again, water dripping from his chin, the door burst open. A revolver stared him in the face.

"What the—?" Marcus couldn't take his eyes off the gun. It wobbled and shook in the hands of a pre-teen boy. "What are you doing?"

The kid—dressed in a huge cop's shirt and a holster—stood about a head shorter than Marcus. In spite of his height, he still had the round, freckled cheeks of a child much younger. Marcus's mother would call him "a solid boy": he blocked the entire doorway. The kid steadied the gun and pointed it at Marcus's face.

Marcus threw his hands up. "Hey, hey, hey … let's take it easy. You just back away from the door real slow, and I'll be on my way. No one gets hurt."

The boy shook his head slowly.

"You don't have to put the gun down. Just back into the hall, and I'll run out the front door. I won't hurt you, I swear." For a moment, Marcus thought of jumping forward to knock the gun out of the kid's hands. But the little bugger's fingers were on the trigger. One quick squeeze and Marcus could wind up dead.

The boy said something Marcus couldn't hear.

"I'm not a burglar," said Marcus. "I used to live here. We moved out just before you moved in. Me and my girlfriend. Is that thing loaded?"

The kid nodded, aimed the gun straight at Marcus's chest.

That was that. Marcus was going to die right here in his old bathroom. At the hands of a kid in a Halloween costume. "Please don't shoot." The revolver slipped a bit lower, pointed at Marcus's groin now. Without thinking, Marcus lowered his hands. "Please! Let's just put the gun down."

The boy shook his head.

"What's your name, kid?"

Whatever the child said came out in short, sharp grunts.

"What?" said Marcus.

"A-alex."

"Alex! Great. Now we're getting somewhere. I told you, I lived in this house right before you moved in. I don't want any trouble. I only came back for my girl's ring."

Somewhere in the house, a cricket chirped.

Marcus looked past Alex. Wondered if he could run faster than Alex could react. But the kid was getting fancy with the gun. He now waved it up and down Marcus's body in the shape of a figure eight.

Marcus backed into the shower and closed the clear glass door. "Please don't shoot! I swear to God, I only came in for, like, three seconds. To get her back her stupid ring. That's all. I'm a normal guy just trying to get his girlfriend back."

Alex stamped his foot for Marcus to be quiet.

There, behind the kid's right shoe, in the crack where the wall and floor tile met—Lisa's ring. Marcus tried as hard as he could not to stare. Lisa was right, the boy could easily take it. Keep it. Alex turned his head a little to see what Marcus was so interested in. He grabbed the ring and held it up, his eyes asking if this was it.

"Yes. Please let me have it."

A slow smile spread across Alex's face.

"Wait, that's Lisa's! You can't keep it—"

As Alex slid the ring into his pocket, he dropped the gun. It crashed to the tile floor, nearly stopping Marcus's heart.

"Get rid of that freaking thing before one of us gets killed!" Marcus's voice echoed off the tile walls. Lisa had been right about the new people in the house keeping the ring. He never should have mocked her. "What are you doing home, anyway? Shouldn't you be in school?"

Alex said something about insulting a cop.

"Cop. Yeah, right. You're a child dressed for Halloween. In April!"

Something in the boy snapped. His eyes flashed bloody murder.

"Where did you get it anyway, your daddy's costume drawer?"

Alex leaped forward in a rage. He grabbed up the gun and shook it at the shower door.

Okay. So the kid was sensitive about his dad. Point to remember in his mission to stay alive. "What is it you want? Want to call 911 on me? Fine. Go ahead. Jail is better than taking a bullet from a …" He almost said "little freak-child," but caught himself. "From a young boy." He pulled out his iPhone and held it out. "Here, use my cell."

"D-d-drop it!"

"You're not going to call 911?"

The boy shook his head.

"What? Why not?"

Alex motioned for him to drop the phone. Marcus was done arguing. He tossed it gently to the floor and watched as the glass face shattered.

There went about $600. He looked at Alex, tired. "What do you want with me?"

Alex moved further into the room, which meant the revolver moved closer to Marcus. Which moved Marcus closer to death.

Keeping the gun pointed at Marcus, Alex sat on the closed toilet. With one hand, he pulled the ring from his pocket and had a good look. He twisted his mouth to one side, deep in thought, then turned his attention back to Marcus.

"My name's Marcus Till. I live just a few blocks away, over on—"

Alex stamped his foot.

After a few moments of silence, Alex stood. Slipped the ring back into his pocket. Using the revolver, he waved Marcus out of the shower. Then, with the barrel nearly pressed into Marcus's back, he forced Marcus down the hall. Into a newly painted bedroom with endangered animal posters on the walls and, in a tank—

"A tarantula? You keep a tarantula?" Marcus didn't know what was worse, the spider or the gun. "You keep a poisonous spider beside your bed?"

"P-pick up B-Boris."

What? "What? I'm not picking up ..."

The revolver returned to Marcus's face.

"Will you give me back the ring if I pick him up? Will you let me go?"

Alex nodded.

Finally. A sign that Marcus would live through the afternoon. He rolled up his sleeves and moved closer to the tank. Even to save his life, Marcus didn't know if he could touch the spider. He needed to play for time. Think. "Can you at least tell me why I'm picking him up?"

The kid, and the gun, took a step toward Marcus. "P-p-pocket him."

What could he do? Marcus sucked in a breath and wrapped his fingers around the furry creature. Held it as gently as he would hold a ticking bomb. Slid it into his jacket pocket. Then closed the zipper, leaving it open enough to allow for breathing. "Okay. I did what you said. Now can I have the ring?"

A look of disgust crossed Alex's face. Marcus might as well have suggested eating the spider for lunch with ice cream. Alex jabbed the gun toward him, then waved toward the door. What could a kidnapping victim do? Marcus did as he was jabbed. He walked out of the house with a gun kissing his back and a spider doing what felt like push-ups in his pocket.

Chapter Eight

The Morrisons' car wasn't in the driveway. Mrs. Morrison had some sort of sickness, like diabetes or kidney trouble—Alex wasn't quite sure. What he did know was that most afternoons, Mr. Morrison drove her to the hospital for care.

The thing about Mr. Morrison was that he was scared to death of spiders. All the kids in the neighbourhood knew the story. Last fall, he had found a big spider tucked right between his trash cans in the garage. The story changed depending upon who told it. Some said it was a deadly brown recluse spider. Others said it was nothing but a harmless daddy longlegs. Either way, everyone said the spider was as big as a man's hand. Morrison himself claimed it was the size of a catcher's mitt.

Didn't really matter. The point was that the spider had scared him into a heart attack. He got better in the hospital, but his heart was badly damaged. The doctors let him out with a warning: no more stress.

Alex made Marcus cross the street. He had tucked the gun under his dad's shirt, but he was still plenty able to poke Marcus with it.

"Are we setting Boris loose now?" asked Marcus. He walked as slowly as he possibly could. When he realized whose driveway they were headed toward, he stopped. "Morrison's place? The guy's a total nut."

The boy grunted his agreement.

"That's what this is about? We're giving the old boy a spider?"

Alex answered with a shrug.

"So this is some kind of revenge." Marcus stared at the Morrison house. Slowly, he started to nod. "I can actually get behind that."

Alex poked him, and they walked through the side gate. The backyard looked different today. Last time Alex had been running flat out. This time he had a chance to really look around. What he saw creeped him out. Patio furniture made of sticks so sharp they could make your eyes bleed from looking at them. A small rubber duck bobbing its beak against a pool's edge, trying to escape. The hedge that had been carved into a snowman family, now had pictures of sad faces hung on each of the tall bushes.

"It's like a horror movie back here," said Marcus. "All we need is scary music."

Alex lifted his eyebrows in agreement and kept Marcus moving toward the house. Marcus didn't need much pushing.

"He's terrified of spiders," Marcus said. "You do know that?"

The kid said nothing.

"He must've done something real bad to you," Marcus went on.

Alex shot him a look that said, *Shut up*. With the gun, he moved Marcus up the steps. At the door, Marcus paused. "Want to see her?"

"Wh-who?"

"Lisa. Can I show you a picture?" When the boy didn't object, Marcus dug into his pocket and pulled out a wallet-sized photo. Held it up.

Alex looked at it a moment too long. Marcus ducked to one side and grabbed for the Smith & Wesson, but Alex was too quick. He jumped back and aimed the gun with two hands. He shook his head angrily, his heart pounding.

"Sorry, sorry!" Marcus held his hands up, backing away. "I won't do it again, okay? I'll help you with the spider. Deal? I help you, you help me. And then we separate. Deal?"

Alex said nothing while he caught his breath. He didn't care that much about Marcus escaping and ratting on him. He could get sent to some kind of kid jail. Didn't really matter. But he would never, ever let Morrison get away with killing his father.

Just as Alex had hoped, the back door was unlocked. Made it nice and easy—no need to break a window to get inside. The kitchen was straight out of the 1950s. Yellow checked curtains, fake marble table with chrome legs, plastic fake-lace place mats. An Elvis Presley clock hung on a wall. Elvis's bent legs danced back and forth with each second. A tin sign said this kitchen was, in fact, "Mom's Diner." But as ugly as the room was, Alex liked it. It had a cozy, grandma appeal.

"I'm sorry," Marcus said, leaning against a bright green fridge. "About before."

Alex shrugged.

"Did you think she was pretty?" Marcus's eyes were bright with hope. Hope that this eleven-year-old kid would agree with what he wanted so badly to believe. "Lisa. She's pretty, right?"

Somehow Marcus looked sadder in this house than he did at Alex's place. His chubby face joined his body with no sign of a neck. The beard looked out of place, that was for sure. Poor guy. In love with a girl so selfish she asked him to commit a crime. *After* she had already walked out on him. Alex smiled. He lowered the gun. "B-beautiful."

Marcus sighed, satisfied. He reached for a banana on the counter and peeled it. Took a bite. "So where do we leave spidey?"

"H-h … h-h-his room. So I can c-c-come back for him. A-a-after." That was the plan. Leave Boris in Morrison's bedroom with the door shut. Then go home and wait for Morrison to return. Wait for the ambulance to show up. Then—once they'd carried the old man's lifeless body away—race back and collect the spider. Feed him an extra-special meal. Two crickets. Maybe three.

Suddenly, Marcus dropped the banana and started pulling at his jacket. "Oh God! I think Boris is loose! I think he's in my shirt!" Bent over, he batted at his belly, tugging his T-shirt out from his pants. Alex dropped the gun and grabbed at Marcus's hands before he hurt the spider. Marcus lost his balance, and the two of them fell to the floor, Marcus still yanking at his clothing.

Alex grabbed Marcus's hands, pinning them to the floor. Something hard pressed into Alex's knee. No sooner had he felt it when a shot rang out. It was so loud Alex thought he'd been hit in the head. Marcus held up his hand, opened his mouth, and let out a silent scream.

A perfect hole edged with a thin black line had appeared in Marcus's hand. They watched the hole go from white to pink to bright red. It filled with blood and then started to leak. Blood dribbled in a thin stream to the floor. Behind the hand, a hole in the fridge door.

"Right through me. The bullet went right through me!" Marcus cried.

"It's o-o-o-o-k-k ...!" said Alex, fighting his panic. "You're going to be f-f-f ..."

"You shot me," Marcus whispered, turning his hand over. "Right through! You shot me right through!"

Alex took Marcus's hand and held it up. If Alex hadn't caused his father's death, this would be the worst thing he'd ever done.

"I'm going to die." Marcus doubled over. "Here in Morrison's kitchen. In front of a dancing Elvis clock."

The bullet went right between the bones, that much was clear. Alex knew from his dad's police talk that Marcus wasn't even going to need a cast. But words stuck on his tongue worse than ever now. So instead of going to the effort of calming Marcus, Alex grabbed a tea towel. He tied it tight around the wound to slow the bleeding.

"Call 911!" said Marcus. "Hurry!"

It wasn't possible. Calling 911 would mean Marcus would go to jail, too. That wouldn't be fair. Marcus was the innocent victim. Okay, maybe not *totally* innocent. But still. Getting shot was enough punishment.

"Please!" Marcus begged. "I don't want to die…"

Alex shook his head. He needed to think like a cop. Look at the Who, What, When, Where, How, and Why. The Who and the What needed no further thought. The When and the Where could not be denied. They needed a How …

"Promise you'll give the ring to Lisa."

And a Why, Alex thought.

"She lives at … oh god, I can't even think with the pain."

Alex looked away from the now blood-soaked tea towel. It made him feel even more guilty and even less able to think. They couldn't call 911 or the police would show up. He knew from his dad that a bullet to the hand wasn't fatal. Not unless it caused a huge loss of blood. But they still had to get Marcus to the hospital. He'd been shot. Emergency room doctors don't care what happened, his dad used to say. They just fix the problem and move the meat. Human meat.

"W-we'll go to em … em … emerg."

"Yes!" Marcus climbed to his feet. He checked his pants pockets with his good hand for his keys and pulled them out.

What about the How? How did the shooting happen? They couldn't show up at the hospital with a bullet hole and no How. Alex thought back to his father emptying the Smith & Wesson on the living room table. "U-un … un-l-loading."

"What?"

"That's the H-how." Of course, the police would check the bullets, if the hospital called them. They'd want to see the gun. It was registered, of course, to Alex's father. "I-it's my d-d-dad's …"

"Okay," said Marcus. "You were checking out your dad's gun when I knocked on the front door. You opened it, gun in hand. I took one look at the gun and insisted on checking to make sure it wasn't loaded. It was. I accidentally shot myself trying to get the bullet out. It's perfect."

"You came f-for your g-g … girlfriend's ring."

"They'll never believe it," said Marcus.

"Th … that you have a g-girlfriend?"

"No! That I just happened by and checked the gun. And, anyway, *you* shot *me* in the hand!"

"Fine. Then y-you broke into my house!"

Marcus held up the bloody towel and turned a shade paler. "I'm getting dizzy. Can we move this along?"

"I'll d-d-d … drive."

"You're, like, eight years old!"

Alex tugged at Marcus's jacket, and a hairy blond ball fell to the floor. They both stared, mouths open. Boris lay perfectly still.

"Oh, no. Your spider's dead."

Alex dropped to his knees. He poked at Boris's lifeless, curled-up legs.

"I am so sorry, Alex," Marcus said. "I couldn't be more sorry. But the thing was crawling all over my body. It was like he was looking for an opening. I just freaked out."

Alex looked at Boris. *How could I have been so cruel as to include an innocent creature in my revenge,* he thought. *If only I hadn't come up with this stupid plan.* Boris would be in the glass tank back at the pet store right now. He'd still be hanging out behind the plastic palm leaf next to the tank full of tiny lizards. His death wasn't Marcus's fault. "A-a-a-accident," Alex said.

They couldn't leave Boris's body here. They had to take him to the hospital, care for him until they could give him a proper burial. Alex grabbed the Kleenex box from the counter. He tore off the top and emptied out half the tissues. He put Boris's little ball-of-yarn body on the bottom tissues and covered him with the others. Then he tucked the cardboard coffin under his arm and held out his hand.

Slowly, Marcus handed over the keys. "You driving is *so* not legal."

Alex took his father's sunglasses from his shirt pocket and pulled them on. "W-w-what part of this d-day is?"

Chapter Nine

Alex explained why driving to the hospital would be simple. He'd watched his parents drive a million times, and he knew a great route that was all side streets. But when he put himself behind the wheel of Marcus's car, Marcus pointed out the problem. His feet didn't quite reach the gas pedal or the brake. Not if he wanted to see where he was going at the same time.

The answer lay in a grocery bag in the back seat. Alex pulled out a four-pack of toilet paper and stuffed it behind his back. Exactly what he needed!

Turned out Alex hadn't learned quite as much as he thought. Marcus had to tell him how to take his foot off the brake and step on the gas. He helped Alex shift from Park into Drive, and the car jerked into motion. Alex guided the vehicle to the middle of the road, as if lanes hadn't been invented yet. The car shook and bumped as they made their way toward the hospital. With any luck, they wouldn't run into the law.

On the cup holder between them sat the spider's Kleenex-box coffin. Neither Alex nor Marcus could so much as glance at it. The guilt was too much.

Marcus kept his hand up, on Alex's orders, to prevent more blood loss. Leaning to one side, forehead pressed to the window, he stared at a passing stop sign. "Rules, Alex. Follow them!" Alex stopped the car with a screech and glared at him. "W-w-want to live or want to d-d … die?"

"You said I couldn't die!"

"I'm el-el-eleven. What do I know?"

For the first time, Marcus noticed the pattern on the tea towel: dancing mice. Even soaked in blood, they looked cheerful. Marcus wondered what the Morrisons would think when they returned. The bullet stuck in the fridge door. The blood on the counters, on the floor, the cupboards. Surely they would call the police. At least the gun wasn't left behind. Alex had had the brains to put it back in the holster.

"You still have Lisa's ring, right?" asked Marcus.
Alex nodded.

The car sprang forward. Marcus felt a warm gush of blood on his palm. He wished, as he had so many times already, that it was the kid who'd been shot. Alex got the car rolling again.

"Why were you after Morrison, anyway? What did he do to you?"

The car slammed to a full stop and they both hit their seat belts hard. A group of three school kids walked past, staring and pointing at Alex behind the wheel.

"Tell me."

Alex rubbed his eyes under the sunglasses. He pressed his lips together and looked around the neighbourhood for a moment. "K-k-k-k … k … k-k-ki …" He waved the question away.

"It's okay. Slow down. The words will come."

"Ki … k-k …"

"He kicked you?"

Alex shook his head. "K … killed my father."

Marcus stared at him.

"H-h-hit and run," said Alex.

The oversized cop shirt. The holster. This was no Halloween costume.

Marcus had heard the story while watching the news with his mother. It had happened late at night, just a few days ago. The cop pulled someone over, and the driver opened the door to climb out. Some idiot went speeding by and took off the driver's door. The driver suffered nicks and scratches. The cop was killed instantly. Left behind a wife and a child. They'd just moved to a new part of town. Kid started a new school. "I don't believe it," he said. "That was your dad?"

Alex didn't react.

"Is Morrison being charged?" Marcus asked.

"Nob … n-nobody believes me." Alex stepped on the gas and sped up smoothly this time.

They drove in silence for a while. Marcus sank lower in his seat. He should have been thinking of Alex, now nearly an orphan. He should have been thinking of his own life. He should have been getting his story straight, the story he would tell at the hospital. But they were too close to her place. Lisa's. All he could think about was … "Turn right on the next street."

Alex jabbed his finger left, toward the hospital.

"Soon. We just have to make a stop first."

Chapter Ten

Alex stopped the car in front of a dumpy grey apartment building. Marcus had been getting more and more nervous the closer they got. He had checked himself in the mirror and smoothed his hair with his good hand. Now he turned to face Alex. He had blood all over his T-shirt. His hand was a dripping mess inside its tea towel. "Give me the ring."

"D-d … don't."

"I want her back. I told you."

Alex stared at Marcus for a minute before fishing the ring out of his pocket. He pushed it into Marcus's good hand.

"Thanks, kid. You're good people." Marcus climbed out of the car and straightened his clothing with his bloody mitt. "How do I look?"

"Like C-C-Clooney." Alex turned off the car. He followed Marcus up a walkway, past dandelions and crabgrass, to a peeling metal door.

"I can do this alone, kid. I don't need a babysitter."

"T-t-tough."

Lisa opened the door like it was three in the morning. Her hair was a mess, as if she'd just climbed out of bed. She scratched her arms through her cotton nightie. Marcus found himself wishing she looked a little better in front of the kid. She glanced down at Marcus's hand and gasped. "What did you do to yourself?"

"Alex here was checking out his dad's gun when I stopped by the old house. I thought, Whoa. Kid. Gun. I gotta do something about this." Marcus gave her an embarrassed half-smile. "So I take the gun away. Make sure it's not loaded and all that. Well, doesn't the damn thing go off, shoot me in the hand." Now he'd made himself sound like a total clumsy idiot. He added quickly, "Could have happened to anyone."

Lisa took Marcus's arm and looked closely at the towel. "Are you serious? You better get to the hospital before you lose too much blood!"

"We're going."

"We should call 911," Lisa said.

Marcus motioned toward Alex. "He's taking me."

"What? He's just a little kid!"

"H-hey!" said Alex.

"He's a great driver. I just wanted to give you …" He opened his good hand and showed Lisa the ring. Maybe it had belonged to her grandma. Maybe the green stone was a real emerald. But it looked smaller and less important than he remembered.

Lisa smiled. She pushed the ring onto her finger and held up her hand. Then she did just what he'd imagined fifty times that day. She wrapped her arms around him and held him tight. Kissed him all over his face. "Oh, thank you, thank you, thank you, baby! I knew you'd do it. I just knew it."

She admired the ring again, then paused. She looked down at her nightie. Blood from Marcus's wounded hand had stained the cotton. She tried to wipe it away, frowning.

Alex caught Marcus's eye. Marcus looked away.

Lisa waved toward her bedroom door. "I'd come with you, but I was right in the middle of … of something. But you could call me after, okay? Let me know what happens, and I'll come right over and see you."

"What?" Marcus said to Alex when they were back in the car. "Lisa didn't know I was going to show up half dead. She was in the middle of something."

Alex nodded.

"Not everyone can just up and go to the Emergency Room, you know. Adults have things they have to do. Work and paying bills and other stuff."

Alex started the engine. Marcus turned on the radio. The hum of the motor mixed with the beat of Guns N' Roses. "Sweet Child O' Mine" had the happy effect of taking away the need to talk. Alex focused on driving; Marcus lay back in his seat.

"She's even prettier in real life, don't you think?" Marcus asked.

The kid sucked in a tired breath.

"You should see her with her hair done. And when she's dressed nice. Looks like a magazine cover model. The first time I saw her, I swear, I thought I'd seen her before on *Cosmo*."

Alex slowed, signalled, and turned right as smoothly as if he'd been driving all his life.

"One time we were getting burgers," Marcus said. "She was wearing this pink dress. Or maybe light purple." His eyes searched the car ceiling for a clue. "Doesn't matter which. The guy behind the counter gives her a free meal. Just because she's so pretty. You ever heard of that happening to anyone? Ever?"

Alex shrugged.

"Mom never liked her," Marcus went on. "But mothers and girlfriends get jealous of each other, I think." He stared out the window. "Craziest thing."

Alex turned into the hospital parking lot. He parked the car sideways across three parking spaces.

"I'll call Lisa after," Marcus said. "Once I get my hand fixed up. She's real sweet. You can't judge a person in three seconds like that." He closed his eyes for a moment. "I don't feel so good."

Alex cut the engine and went around to open Marcus's door. He helped Marcus to his feet, and together they started toward the Emergency Room doors. Marcus, from fear or blood loss or pain, couldn't walk very straight. He leaned on Alex for support.

"I'm going to marry that girl," he said.

They were almost at the door when Alex stopped. His face hardened, and he pointed at an old red Ford Taurus. Picked up a rock. Before Marcus could stop him, Alex threw it at the windshield. The rock flew off to the side and skipped across the hood of a brand new SUV.

Marcus grabbed Alex's arm. "What are you doing?"

"It's h-h-his—that's M-m … Morrison's car!"

Marcus let the boy go and circled the car, looking closely at the passenger side. He bent over the bumpers and tires. He checked the head and tail lights. Finally, he checked out the chip Alex had just made in the windshield.

Alex, collapsed on a bench, started to cry, his shoulders shaking with each sob. His dad's sunglasses fell to his feet, and Marcus picked them up. He wrapped his arm around the boy and held him close. A woman with a handful of flowers stopped to ask if they needed help. Marcus waved her on.

Five minutes later, maybe ten, Alex looked up. His face was puffy and wet, and tears stuck his eyelashes together in clumps. When he started to speak, his voice came out thin and high. "I-it's my fault. I'm the reason Morrison went after my d-dad. I wrecked the stupid bushes. My d-dad would be at work right now…" He looked down and touched the shirt. "He'd be wearing this if I hadn't cut across Old Man Morrison's lawn."

Marcus made Alex look him in the eye. "It's not your fault, Alex."

"Is so."

"It was just an accident. A rotten, sucky, piece-of-shit accident. Just like the gun going off. Just like the spider."

"You weren't there. D-dad went over to Morrison's and—"

"Alex. Morrison didn't do it."

"You don't know anything. He did so!"

Marcus stood the boy up, led him to the front of the car, and walked him around it. "There's no damage. Not even a dent. It isn't possible for this car to have taken the door off another vehicle with no damage."

"That proves nothing. Morrison got it fixed. Repainted." Alex wiped away his tears, leaving a faint smear of Marcus's blood on his cheek.

"The paint on his car isn't fresh. The only damage on that car was caused by a rock to the windshield. Just now. The rock you threw." He stared at Alex. "What happened to your dad was a terrible accident. A rotten, sucky, piece-of-shit accident that never should have happened. But it did. Life blows sometimes, and there's not much you can do about it. You can't possibly control all the good and bad that happens. I mean this in the nicest way possible: not everything is about you."

"Why don't you shut up!" Alex dug his fingernails into his jeans. "What do you know, anyway? You're just some goof-off with a crappy girlfriend. A girlfriend so crappy she can't even stand that you bled on her nightgown. Why would I listen to you?"

Marcus didn't speak right away. He held his bad hand to his chest, and pain tore through the hand and into his wrist. "Okay. I'm going inside before I pass out here in the parking lot."

"Go. I never want to see you again. You killed my spider."

Marcus turned away, leaving Alex to study the rust and dead bugs on Morrison's car. But first, he handed the kid a twenty. "Hide the gun and holster in my car. Go over there to the exit and wave at a cab. Get home before your mother starts to worry."

Chapter Eleven

Marcus lay on his side in the hospital recovery room. On the pale green wall was a framed picture of a sailboat floating in water that sparkled in the sunlight. A happy image, but it didn't take his mind off the machines beeping behind his bed. When the phone rang, he picked it up with his good hand. "Hello," he said.

"They told me they had to operate," said Lisa. "Are you okay?"

Marcus looked at his hand, bandaged properly now. No more tea towel. No more blood-soaked dancing mice. He felt drunk and swimmy, as if underwater. For a moment, he thought he could be dying. But no. He was all drugged up.

Everything after he left Alex in the parking lot was a blur. He must have fainted after walking into the Emergency Room. All he could remember was telling the nurse he'd been cleaning a gun and it went off. Being happy no one questioned his story. Then the world went black. Now, here he was with wires snaked under his hospital gown. And here was Lisa on the phone. "Feeling okay now, all in all," he told her.

"I'm so sorry, Marcus. They said you'd be in the hospital all night. I'm packing a bag so I can come take care of you. The nurse said I can sleep in the comfy chair in your room. I called your mom. She's going to pick me up. I really miss you, baby."

Marcus heard a squeak behind him and rolled onto his back. There, on the comfy chair, still in his father's shirt, sat Alex. He waved shyly.

"Lisa?" said Marcus. "I have to go. But don't worry about coming. I'm fine."

"What do you mean? I'm all packed. I'm ready to leave."

"I'll call when I get home." *Or maybe I won't*, he didn't say.

When Marcus hung up, Alex came to the bedside. Set the Kleenex box on the blanket. Ugh.

He'd forgotten about killing Alex's spider. But before he could tell Alex to take the coffin away, he noticed a fuzzy blond leg. It pawed at the inside of the box. "He made it." Marcus sat up so fast the room spun. "Like a hairy little soldier."

"Like a hairy little soldier."

"I thought I killed him."

"You didn't kill anyone." Alex shoved his hands in his pockets. The gun and holster were gone. "It was a rotten, sucky, piece-of-shit accident. Not everything's about you, you know."

Laughing softly, Marcus let himself fall back onto the pillows. "Is that so, Sergeant?"

"As soon as you're done lying around here, I've got a new plan."

Marcus groaned. "I'm afraid to ask."

"Ever been on a cricket hunt?"

Good ⧄ Reads

Discover Canada's Bestselling Authors with Good Reads Books

Good Reads authors have a special talent—
the ability to tell a great story, using clear language.

Good Reads can be purchased as eBooks, downloadable
direct to your mobile phone, eReader or computer.
Some titles are also available as audio books.

To find out more, please visit
www.GoodReadsBooks.com

The Good Reads project is sponsored by
ABC Life Literacy Canada.

Grass Roots Press

Good Reads Series

Coyote's Song by Gail Anderson-Dargatz

The Stalker by Gail Anderson-Dargatz

The Break-In by Tish Cohen

Tribb's Troubles by Trevor Cole

In From the Cold by Deborah Ellis

New Year's Eve by Marina Endicott

Home Invasion by Joy Fielding

The Day the Rebels Came to Town by Robert Hough

Picture This by Anthony Hyde

Listen! by Frances Itani

Missing by Frances Itani

Shipwreck by Maureen Jennings

The Picture of Nobody by Rabindranath Maharaj

The Hangman by Louise Penny

Easy Money by Gail Vaz-Oxlade

Coyote's Song

by Gail Anderson-Dargatz

Sara used to be a back-up singer in a band. She left her singing career to raise a family. She is content with being a stay-at-home mom. Then, one Saturday, Sara's world changes.

Sara and her family go to an outdoor music festival. There, on stage, Sara sees Jim, the lead singer from her old band. He invites her to sing with him. Being on stage brings back forgotten feelings for Sara—and for Jim. And Sara's husband Rob sure doesn't like what he sees.

Sara also sees something else: a coyote. Learn how Coyote, the trickster spirit, turns Sara's life upside down.

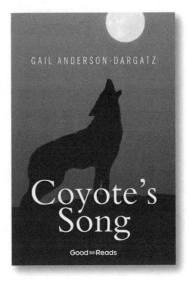

About the Author

 As a child, Tish Cohen knew she wanted to write novels, but didn't have the nerve. As an adult, Tish finally took the risk and began to write. Today, she is the bestselling author of six books. Tish also writes articles for *The Globe and Mail* and *The National Post*. She lives in Toronto with her two sons.

Also by Tish Cohen:

Novels for Adults
The Truth About Delilah Blue
Inside Out Girl
Town House

Novels for Younger Readers
Switch
The One and Only Zoë Lama
The Invisible Rules of the Zoë Lama
Little Black Lies (forthcoming)

You can visit Tish's website at
www.tishcohen.com